Content

 6A Assessm

 **6B Assessment**

6A written by
David Grant

6A illustrated by
Andy Stephens
and **Dylan Gibson**

6B written by
David Clayton

6B illustrated by
Peter Richardson

Series editor **Dee Reid**

Heinemann
Part of Pearson

Characters

Kris

Jake

Kelly

Tricky words

- sighed
- brilliant
- website
- already
- stolen
- pointing
- happened
- smiled

Read these words to the student. Help them with these words when they appear in the text.

Introduction

Kris and Jake are best mates. Kelly is in their year at school. She is a computer genius. One day, Kris and Jake were round at Kelly's house when Kris let out a big sigh. He had got a phone off a website just the day before but it was already busted. Kelly checked out the website. She reckoned all the phones were stolen. Then she found out something else – the man who owned the website was her neighbour!

Nicked!

Kris and Jake were round at Kelly's house.
Kelly and Jake were playing a game on the computer.
"Want a go?" said Kelly to Kris.
Kris just sighed.
"What's the matter?" asked Jake.
"I got a brilliant phone off a website yesterday,"
said Kris. "But it's busted already."

"Show me the website," said Kelly.
Kris showed her.
"This is a really nasty website," said Kelly.
"I bet these are all stolen phones."

4

She started typing on the computer.
"Look!" said Kelly, pointing at the scre
"That website is run by the guy next d
That's his house over there!" she said.

Kris and Jake looked.
"I'm going to get my money back," whi
He looked angry.
"Are you coming?" he whispered to Jak
"OK," said Jake.

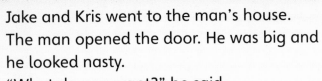

Jake and Kris went to the man's house.
The man opened the door. He was big and
he looked nasty.
"What do you want?" he said.
"I got a phone off your website and it's busted,"
said Kris. "I want my money back."

The man laughed and picked up a bat.
"Ask me again," he said.
Kris looked at Jake. They both made a run for it!

The next day, Kris and Jake went round to Kelly's house.

They told her what had happened.

"You idiots," said Kelly. "I've got a better idea to sort him out."

Kelly started typing on her computer.

"What are you doing?" asked Kris.

"I'm hacking into his computer," said Kelly.

"Amazing!" said Kris.

Templates

"He's got loads of emails! They're all about phones from his website. They all say the phones don't work," said Kelly.

From	Subject
David@skymail.com	Broken Phone!
Mal@mymail.com	Phone not working!
Jane@	
John@	
Debs(	
Daz@	
June(	
Greg@mailworld.com	Please ca... e my money back?
Zak@newweb.com	Broken phon... respond.

New message _ 🗗 ✕

Subject: Need more phones...

Steal more phones for me.
See you tonight at my place.

David@skymail.com

Broken Phone, still not working. I want my money back!
David

"And look at this email!" said Kelly, pointing at the screen. "The guy next door is telling someone to steal more phones to go on his website!"

"What are you doing now?" asked Kris.
"I'm sending his emails on to the police,"
said Kelly. "I'm sure they would like to read them."

The next day, Kelly was in her room when she heard shouting. She went to see what was happening.

The police were coming out of the man next door's house.
One of them had loads of phones.
The man next door was in the back of a police car.
Kelly smiled.

Text comprehension

Literal comprehension
p3 Why did Kris sigh?
p5 What did Kelly discover about the website?
p5 What did Kris decide to do?
p7 How did the man scare off Kris and Jake?
p10 What was Kelly's idea?

Inferential comprehension
p5/8 How can you tell Kelly is a computer genius?
p7/9 How can you tell the neighbour is a criminal?
p12 Why did Kelly smile at the end?

Personal response
- Do you think it was a good idea to go round to the man's house?
- Do you think Kris was foolish to buy a cheap phone off the internet?

Spelling challenge

Study these words for one minute. Then write them from memory.

Phonically regular

morning   clever   yesterday

family   running

Irregular

friend   people   someone   heard   you're

Ha! Ha! Ha!

What do prisoners use to call each other?

Cell phones!

Characters

Joe

Man in a silver suit

Man in a dark suit

Tricky words

- explosives
- simulator
- security
- gasped

- followed
- corridor
- covered
- programmed

Read these words to the student. Help them with these words when they appear in the text.

Introduction

Joe knew there was something strange going on in Moon City. He had seen trucks carrying explosives near the mines. He had seen a simulator rocket set to target Earth and he had seen a secret control room in a tunnel far below the city. Joe decided to tell Moon Security about all the things he had seen.

Alien Attack!

Something strange is going on in Moon City, thought Joe.

He had seen strange lights near the mines and trucks carrying explosives. He had seen a simulator rocket set to target Earth. He had seen a secret control room in a tunnel far below the city.

What does it all mean? thought Joe.

Joe went to Moon Security. He told them about the things he had seen. "It's OK," said the man. "We have everything under control."

But as Joe turned to go, he saw a strange look in the man's eyes.

Joe hid behind the door and watched the man from Moon Security. Then he gasped. The man was pulling a mask off his face. Under the mask was an alien!

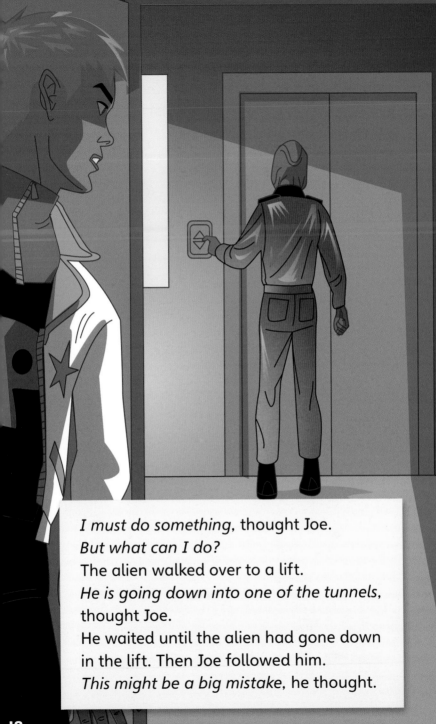

I must do something, thought Joe.
But what can I do?
The alien walked over to a lift.
He is going down into one of the tunnels, thought Joe.
He waited until the alien had gone down in the lift. Then Joe followed him.
This might be a big mistake, he thought.

When he got out of the lift, Joe looked down the corridor and saw a door.
It was the control room where he had seen the map of Earth! Joe's heart was thumping as he crept towards the room.

The big map of Earth was covered with lights by each city.
A huge alien was talking to aliens in silver suits. "Everything is set," he said. "The explosives have been checked at the old mines. The rockets are loaded and programmed to hit Earth. This is the end for all people, and aliens will take control!"

I must stop them! thought Joe.
Behind the huge alien was a big switch.
Joe ran at the alien and knocked him
out of the way.
As he turned off the big switch,
Joe heard the buzz of space guns.
Now they will get me, he thought, *I'm dead!*

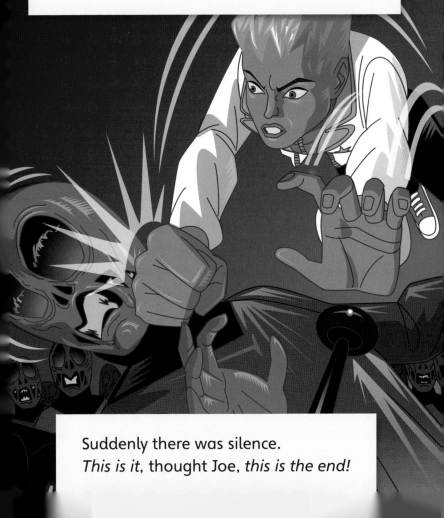

Suddenly there was silence.
This is it, thought Joe, *this is the end!*

But nothing happened.
He looked up and saw the man in the dark suit
who had helped him out of the mine.
Behind him were other people in dark suits.
The aliens were dead on the floor.

Joe had been right. Strange things *had*
been going on in Moon City.
"How did you find out what was going on?"
Joe asked the man in the dark suit.
"We knew what was going on all along,"
said the man, "but you kept getting in the way!"
But it was me that stopped the aliens in the end!
thought Joe.

Quiz ///////////////////////////

Literal comprehension

p15 What was the simulator rocket set to do?

p15 Where was the secret control room?

p17 Why did Joe gasp?

p20 What was on the map of Earth?

p21 What did Joe do to the alien?

Inferential comprehension

p16 Why did the man in Moon Security say they had everything under control?

p21 Why did Joe think it was the end?

p23 Is the man in the dark suit pleased with Joe?

Personal response

- Do you think Joe was brave?
- Were the aliens clever?

Spelling challenge

Study these words for one minute. Then write them from memory.

Phonically regular

**nothing   beginning   surprised
another   suddenly**

Irregular

**somebody   laughed   wouldn't
through   everything**

Now try to spell them!

Ha! Ha! Ha!

How did the astronaut serve dinner in outer space?

On flying saucers!